Minecraft: The Ultimate Survival Handbook

Emerson Kirby

Table of Contents

Introduction..3

Learning the Basics in Survival Mode 7

  Paying Attention to Food and Hunger.................10

  Be Aware of the Dangers in Night Time 15

  Understanding Death and Re-spawning...............18

  Minecraft Mobs and Monsters............................23

Identify your Biome...31

  Snowy Biomes 33

  Cold Biomes..35

  Lush Biomes...38

Dry Biomes 43

Surviving the First Day in Minecraft 46

Learning to Collect Resources 48

The Basics of Crafting 52

The Basics of Smelting 56

Understanding Heat and Light...............................60

Crafting and Upgrading Your Tools and Weapons64

Building Your First Shelter 67

Introduction

Launched in 2009, Minecraft is among the most beloved games on the Internet. With a new Story mode launched as well, the game shows it keeps on growing.

Simple in design and structure, Minecraft has been played on a global level. With five different game modes, available on different platforms it's easy to take your pick and play the mode which suits you best.

With various gaming platforms available, Minecraft launched an Android version on October 7th, 2011 shortly followed with an iOS version on November 17th, 2011. And on May 9th, 2012, Minecraft released a version for Xbox 360 as well.

Among the game modes, you now get Creative, Survival, Adventure, Spectator and Hardcore.

While Minecraft is renowned for its Creative mode, the builds you can make in it are awesome, if you want a bit of a challenge, the other story modes might be the ones for you.

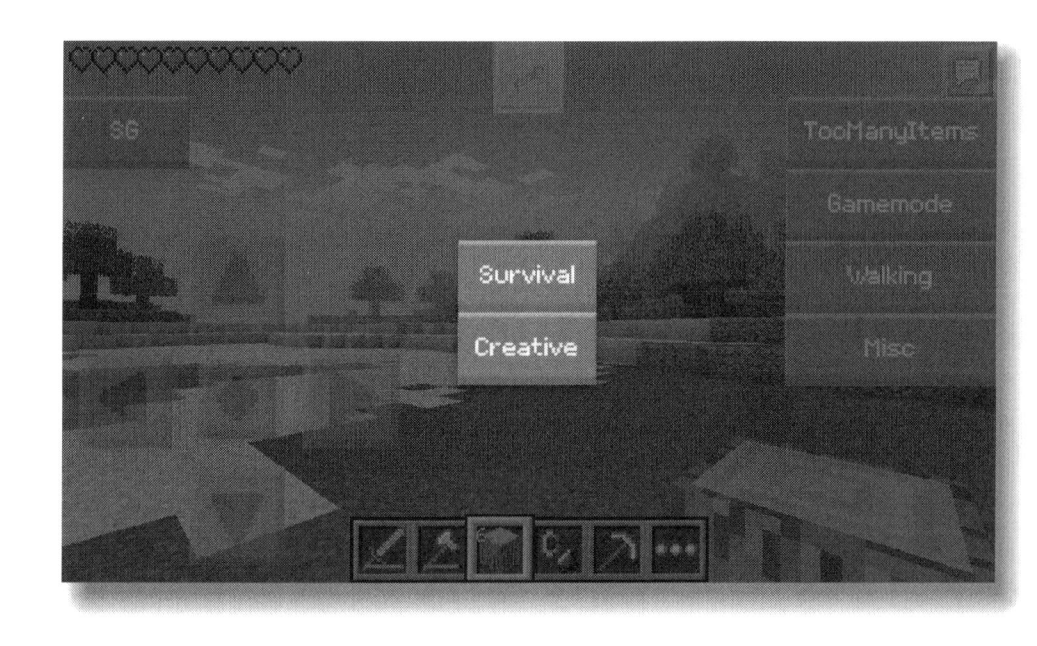

If you're still a beginner, the Survival mode would be a better option before you graduate on to Adventure, Spectator and Hardcore. With the help of this eBook, we're going to show how easy it is to survive in Survival mode.

Learning the Basics in Survival Mode

While you might be tempted into taking Survival mode lightly, don't be fooled. With mobs and monsters around which can harm you easily, Survival mode is definitely challenging for many players.

Luckily, there aren't many basics other than the fact that you have to create a habitable environment for your character.

BASICS

For this purpose, you're going to indulge in activities such as farming, breeding, crafting smelting, mining and other actions which all contribute to having a happy Minecraft life. Minecraft also follows a day/night cycle which lasts for 20 minutes.

This means that spending an hour on Minecraft means you experienced 3 days in Minecraft and spending a day on the game can mean 2 and a half months in Minecraft.

Apart from this, you also have to pay attention to the fact that Minecraft incorporates real world physics into the game. If you build something which is lopsided, it will experience the pull of gravity and collapse.

This makes building a more time consuming process as well but it all contributes towards making the game play more interesting.

Paying Attention to Food and Hunger

In Creative mode, players don't experience food and hunger while in Survival mode, if you don't pay attention, you are going to starve to death.

All players have a health bar which diminishes over time, particularly, when you are performing actions or sprinting, your health bar will slowly decrease.

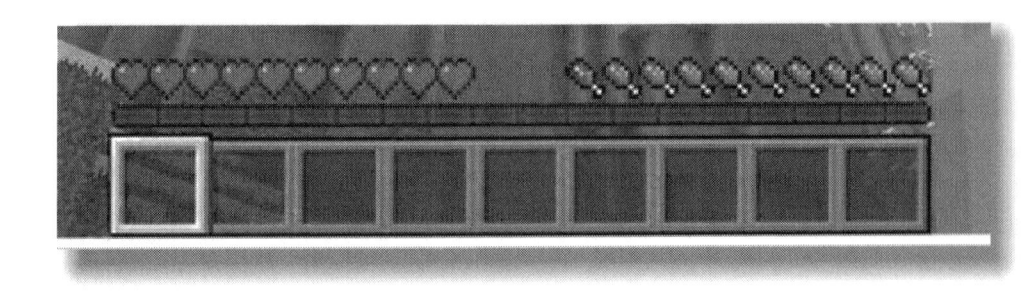

If your health bar goes below 90%, it won't regenerate automatically and if it goes beyond 30% then you won't be able to perform certain actions.

You won't starve to death as long as you aren't playing the hard mode for Survival but it will leave you extremely vulnerable as well.

Minecraft Food Pyramid

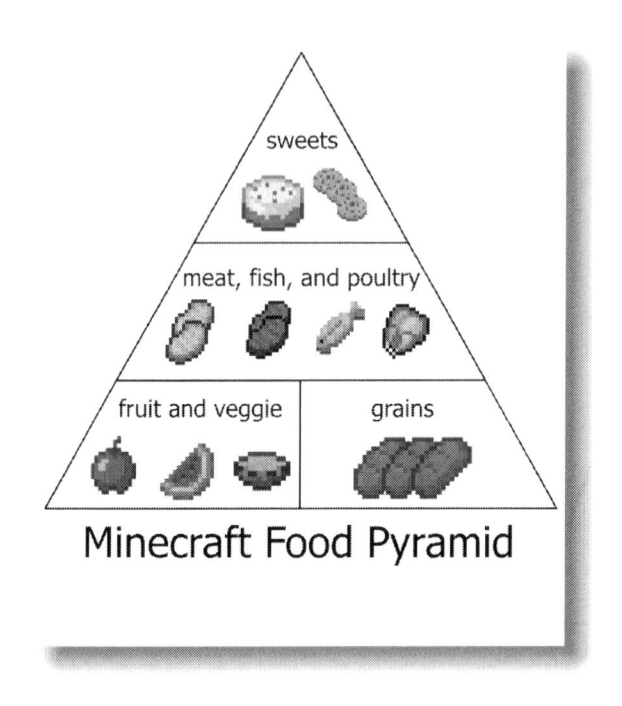

Food can be gathered and harvested from your surroundings. You can raise crops with the help of seeds and you can also kill mobs like sheep, cows, chicken and others to get meat, fish and poultry.

All raw food items should be cooked in the furnace before you consume them. This gives your higher health points and also reduces the chances of your player getting sick.

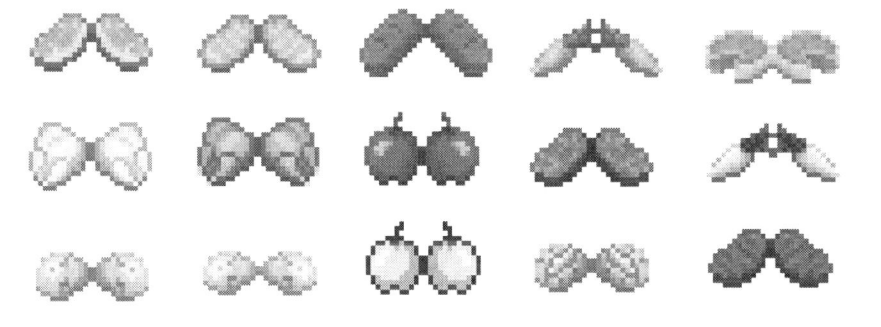

Raw chicken, in particular will give you food poisoning. Other raw foods like beef can be consumed as is but they give higher health points once they are cooked.

Be Aware of the Dangers in Night Time

In Survival modes, night time is not going to be dangerous. This is when the monsters come out to play and they can cause serious damage, particularly if you have no armor or weapons.

Hunting monsters might seem exciting but it's the easiest way to die at the start of the game.

The best thing to do is to stay in a well-lit area or shelter. Place torches, glow stones, or even jack-o-lanterns around your house to keep the monsters at bay.

Torches are easier to make since you just need wooden sticks and charcoal or coal to make them with so craft a good supply as quickly as possible for night time.

Understanding Death and Re-spawning

In Minecraft, it is possible for you to die once your health bar is completely depleted. When this happens, you will be re-spawned but there is a down side to it.

If you die, anything you are wearing or carrying in your inventory gets scattered while your re-spawn might happen anywhere else on the map.

This happens every time you die and you will have to start all over again. The only way to break this cycle is to craft a bed and sleep in it.

This will become your re-spawn point and prevent you from being shipped off to other points of the map.

The best thing to do is to build a shelter around your spawn point. This makes sure that you don't suffer from any sneak attacks by monsters that may be lurking around your re-spawn point.

If you die really far away from your re-spawn site, the items you dropped will disappear within 5 minutes unless you are 180 blocks away from them.

Even then, it can take some time to collect them, particularly if you died at night because you will re-spawn without any armor or weapons.

The monsters in Minecraft arc particularly resourceful and they can guard your items or even use the weapons against you.

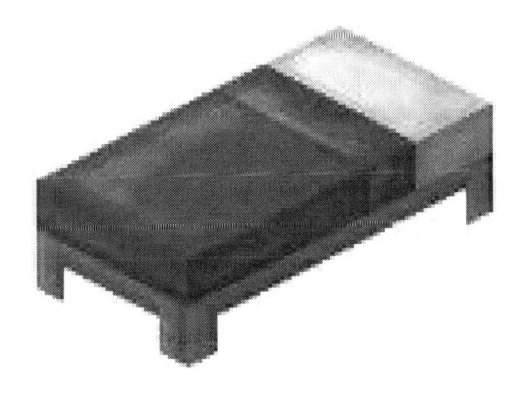

With a bed, you can sleep in it in a safe shelter which means that if you die, you will re-spawn in your bed and your items won't disappear.

To make a bed you will need three blocks of wool and three blocks of wood so it may take you time, but once you have the resources, start crafting immediately.

Minecraft Mobs and Monsters

Minecraft has different mobs aka mobile hordes which will be your bane and provide a challenge in your game.

While most are only active during the night, some can spawn during the day in any dark and gloomy areas as well. Weapons like swords, bow and arrows and axes can be used to kill them.

Some monsters also drop resources which can be used in crafting and other recipes. With three realms, Minecraft has plenty of monsters.

While all drop resources, some mobs can harm you as soon as they catch sight of you, such as the:

- Creeper,
- Zombie,
- Skeleton,
- Pig Men,
- Silverfish,
- Magma,
- Zombie Pig Men,
- Ghast,

- Cave Spider,
- Spider,
- Blaze,
- Witch,
- Zombie Villager,
- Wither Skeleton,
- Spider Jockey
- Endermen.

Some mobs like the Wolf, Zombie Pigmen, Endermen and the Iron Golem will not harm you unless you provoke them.

Slime	Spider	Spider Jockey	Witch

Wither Skeleton	Zombie	Zombie Villager

Enderman	Wolf	Zombie Pigman

While there are harmful mobs in the game, you will also come across passive mobs which don't harm you. These provide players with important resources like meat, leather, milk and more.

This mob includes:

- Sheep,

- Cows,

- Chicken,

- Bats,

- Mooshrooms (Mushroom Cows)

- Chicken,

- Squid,

- Ocelot,
- Pig,
- Villager,

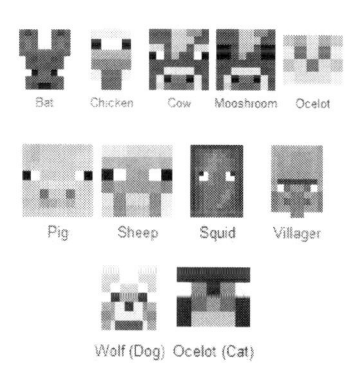

Bat Chicken Cow Mooshroom Ocelot

Pig Sheep Squid Villager

Wolf (Dog) Ocelot (Cat)

The Ocelot and Wolf are tamable and will turn into a Dog and Cat if they are given raw chicken or fish.

Other mobs like the Sheep, Chicken, and Cow etc can be tamed with wheat and will follow players into different corrals. Once you have herded them, you can breed more animals.

Identify your Biome

The kind of resources you have access to will be greatly influenced by the biome you enter once you start the game.

Since you always start on the Overworld, you will get access to geographically correct landscapes which are known as biomes.

Ideally, forest and jungle biomes are the best since they give you quick access to wood which will be your biggest need when you are starting out.

The following are some of the biomes you can find

and the resources they provide:

Snowy Biomes

In snowy biomes, it snows regardless of the height and there's not much foliage available.

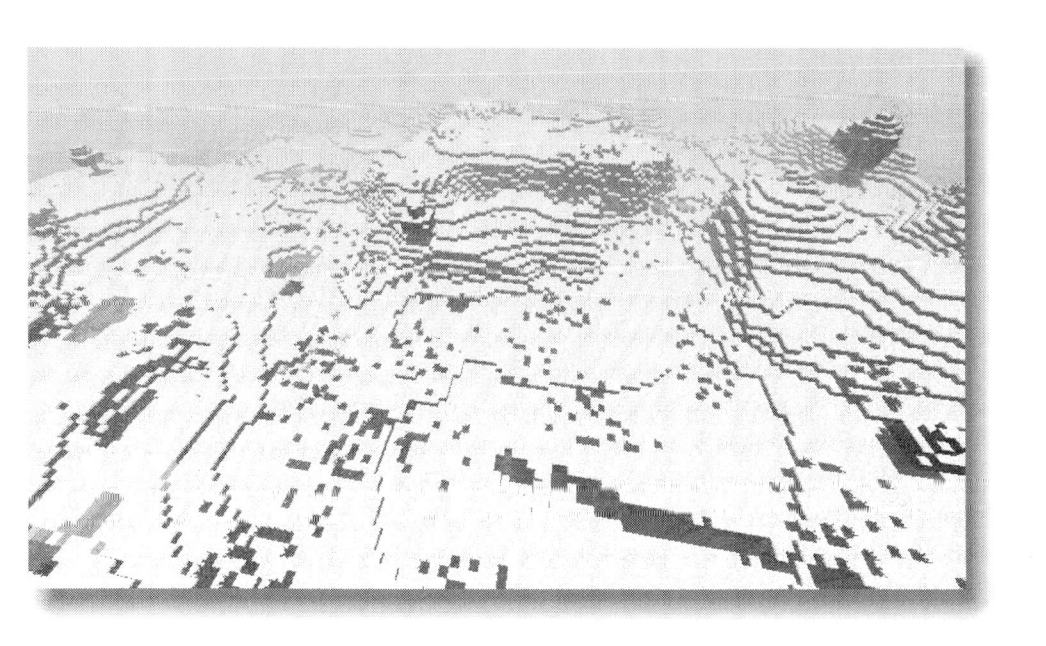

You can come across different variants such as:

- Frozen River: Ice, sand, water and clay

- Ice Plains: Oak, spruce, ice, snowfall and snow

- Ice Plains (Spike): Snow, ice, snow blocks, packed ice

- Cold Beach: Sand, snow and snowfall

- Cold Taiga: Ice, snowfall, spruce, snow, wolves and flowers

- Cold Taiga (M): Snow, wolves, snowfall, ferns and spruce

Cold Biomes

These biomes experience snowfall at a certain height. It does rain here occasionally though.

You can come across different variants such as:

- Extreme Hills: Spruce, flowers, oak, emerald ore and monster egg
- Extreme Hills (M): Oak, gravel, spruce, and snow
- Taiga: Wolves, spruce, fern and flowers
- Taiga (M): Sheep, spruce, fern and flowers
- Mega Taiga: Ferns, podzol, wolves, spruce, mushrooms and moss stones
- Mega Spruce Taiga: Ferns, podzol, spruce, mushrooms and moss stones
- Extreme Hills+: Spruce, stone and oak

- Extreme Hills+ (M): Spruce, stone, gravel and oak
- Stone Beach: Stone

Lush Biomes

These biomes don't experience a lot of snowfall but at certain heights you can find snow. Rain is experienced occasionally and there is plenty of green foliage and shrubbery.

You can come across different variants such as:

- Plains: Tall grass, horses, flowers, NPC villages and grass
- Plains (M): Tall grass, flowers, horses and grass
- Sunflower Plains: Sunflowers, horses and grass
- Forest: Oak, flowers, birch, wolves and mushrooms
- Flower Forest: Oak, flowers, birch and mushrooms
- Swamp Land: Oak, vines, lily pads, witches, water, mushrooms, slime, clay and giant mushrooms

- Swamp Land: Oak, vines, lily pads, witches, water, mushrooms, slime, clay and giant mushrooms
- River: Water, clay and sand
- Beach: Sand
- Jungle: Jungle temples, trees, ferns, cocoa beans, melons, ocelots and flowers
- Jungle (M): Jungle temples, trees, ferns, cocoa beans, melons, ocelots and flowers
- Jungle Edge: Jungle trees, ferns, cocoa beans, melons, ocelots, vines and flowers

- Jungle Edge (M): Jungle trees, ferns, cocoa beans, melons, ocelots, vines and flowers
- Birch Forest: Birch and flowers
- Birch Forest (M): Birch and flowers
- Birch Forest Hills: Birch, grass, cows and flowers
- Birch Forest Hills (M): Birch, grass, cows and flowers
- Roofed Forest: Dark oak, rose bushes, mushrooms and giant mushrooms
- Roofed Forest (M): Dark oak and giant mushrooms

- Mushroom Island: Mushrooms, mooshrooms, giant mushrooms and no hostile mobs
- Mushroom Island Shore: Mushrooms, mooshrooms, giant mushrooms and no hostile mobs

Dry Biomes

These biomes don't experience snow or rain at all.

Not a lot of green foliage is found and trees are also harder to find.

You can come across different variants such as:

- Desert: Dead bushes, sand, cacti, sandstones, sugar cane, desert temple, desert stone and NPC villages

- Desert (M): Water, sand, cactus and sugar cane

- Savanna: Acacia, NPC villages, horses, sheep, cows and tall grass

- Savanna (M): Acacia and tall grass

- Mesa: Red sand, hardened clay, colored clay, red sandstones, gold ore, mineshafts and dead bushes

- Mesa Bryce: Red sand, hardened clay, colored clay, red sandstones and dead bushes

Even if you don't end up on a biome which yields many resources, you can always travel to other biomes in order to get them.

Surviving the First Day in Minecraft

Now that you are aware of your surroundings at least, let's start focusing on making your player safe and secure.

The first day is always the most important one. You may be in a biome which looks perfectly safe but once the mobs come out; your player will be in a lot of trouble.

Once you survive the first day, the others will go smoothly over time. The first thing you have to do is to collect resources.

Learning to Collect Resources

Identify the biome you are in and look for visible resources such as trees and stones, tall grass and any other animals. Tall grass drops seeds which are important for when you start farming for your own crops.

You may also find loose items like mushrooms, apples and other resources while you're exploring. Almost all resources that you come across can be used in crafting, smelting, enchanting or brewing.

The first thing you have to do is to collect wood. Since you don't have any tools at the moment, the best way to do that is to knock on a tree until a block of wood drops down.

Collect as much wood as you possibly can since you will need it to build items like wooden tools, doors, torches, chests and more. When you are just starting out, wood blocks are going to be your best friends.

Once you think you have enough, go back and chop some more to double the amount.

This will be a time consuming process but keep an eye on the clock. You don't want to get caught out when it's dark and the only thing you have done up till now is collect wood blocks.

The Basics of Crafting

Once you have the wood blocks, start crafting with the help of your inventory crafting grid. You need wood planks and lots of them.

Throughout the game, you will rely heavily on your crafting table so make one as soon as possible. You will need four planks of wood to create a crafting table.

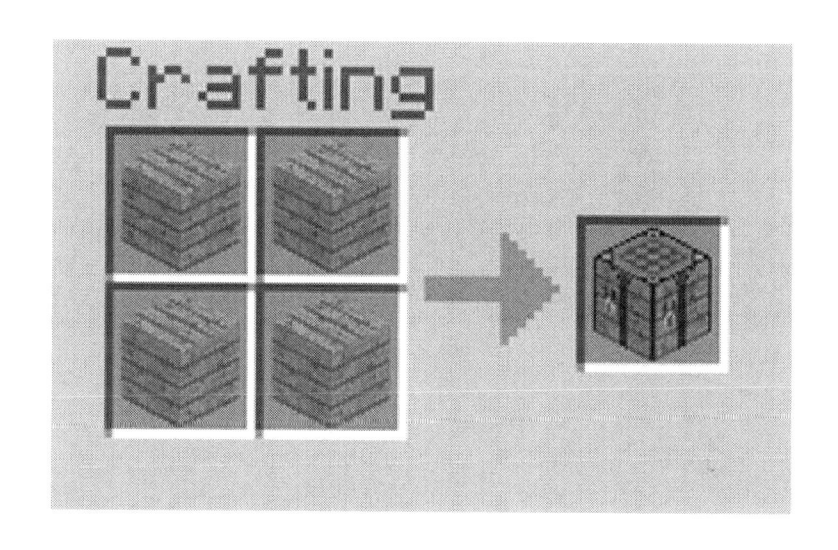

While your inventory will have a built in crafting grid which will allow you to craft simple items, you are still going to need a crafting table for more complex builds.

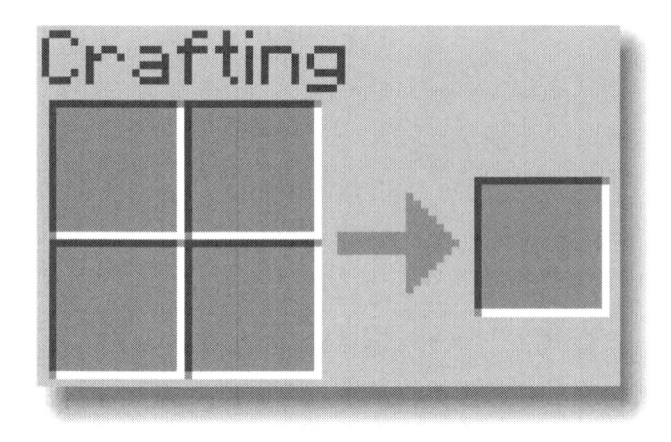

Once the crafting table is ready, get to work.

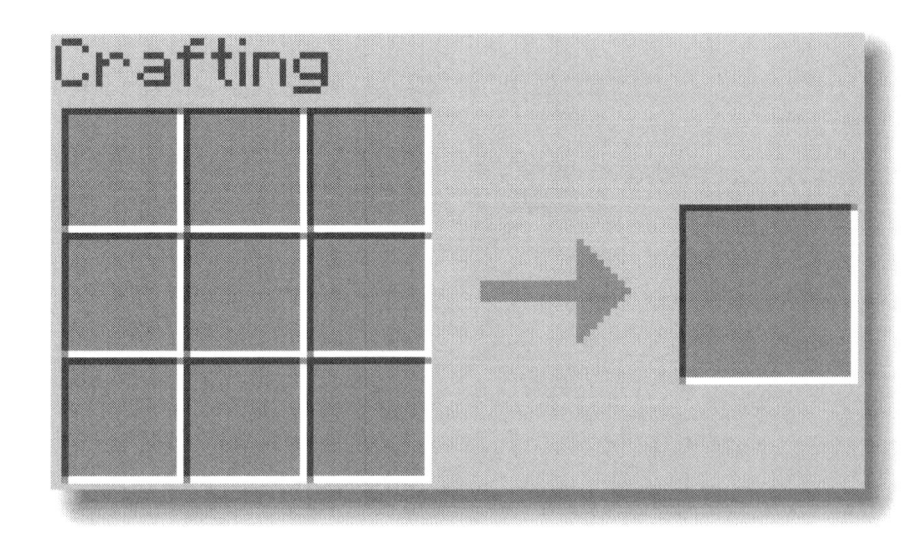

The first things you need to craft are an axe, a pick axe, a wooden sword, a shovel and some wooden sticks as well for torches. Axes make it easier to collect more wood and wooden pick axes also make mining faster.

Once you can mine and cut more easily, collecting resources will go smoother as well.

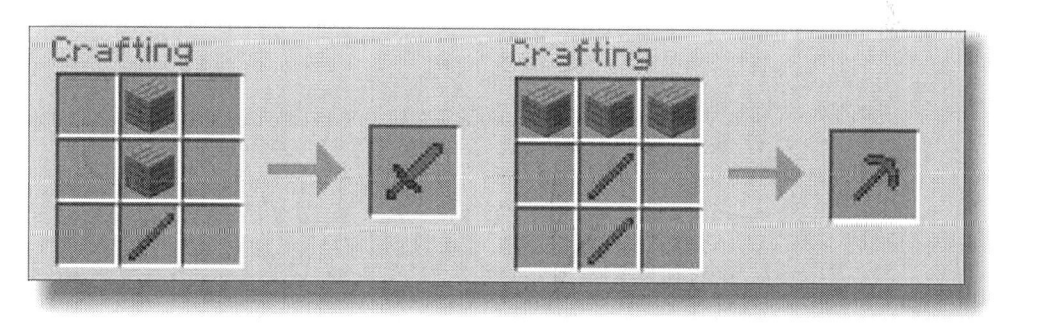

The Basics of Smelting

Once you have access to a pick axe, you need to start mining for stone.

With stone, you can not only craft sturdier tools and weapons but you can also create a furnace which will help you process any ores you mine.

Ores need to be refined in the furnace to get materials like iron, tin, gold and other precious metals which you can use.

Moreover, you will also be able to build better structures as well as cook raw food items for yourself. Furnaces also require fuel so you will need coal and charcoal if you plan to smelt.

Charcoal can be easily made by burning 4 blocks of wood to yield one lump of charcoal. Once you have charcoal or coal, you can combine it with a wooden stick to create a torch.

Understanding Heat and Light

You will need coal and charcoal in abundance, particularly when smelting or cooking something. If you haven't found any coal as yet, you can burn wood to make charcoal.

Each piece of charcoal will smelt around 8 items so pay attention to this factor when you are smelting or cooking anything in the furnace.

You can also make wooden torches with the help of coal so do so as quickly as possible. Only make charcoal if you cannot find any coal since wood is required for a lot of other items as well.

Moreover, if you have gotten stone tools, you can burn your wooden tools in the furnace as well since stone tools will be more efficient as compared to them and you won't need them.

However, one wooden tool will only provide enough fuel to smelt or cook one item only. If you have charcoal and coal, you should opt to save the coal lumps and burn the charcoal first.

Any torches you make will also be made in batches of 8 since one lump can smelt 8 items, this gives you access to a lot of torches so you can easily light up your shelter properly.

Crafting and Upgrading Your Tools and Weapons

As you collect more resources, you can smelt and craft better tools as well. You will start out with wooden items but once you can mine for stone, you can create stone tools.

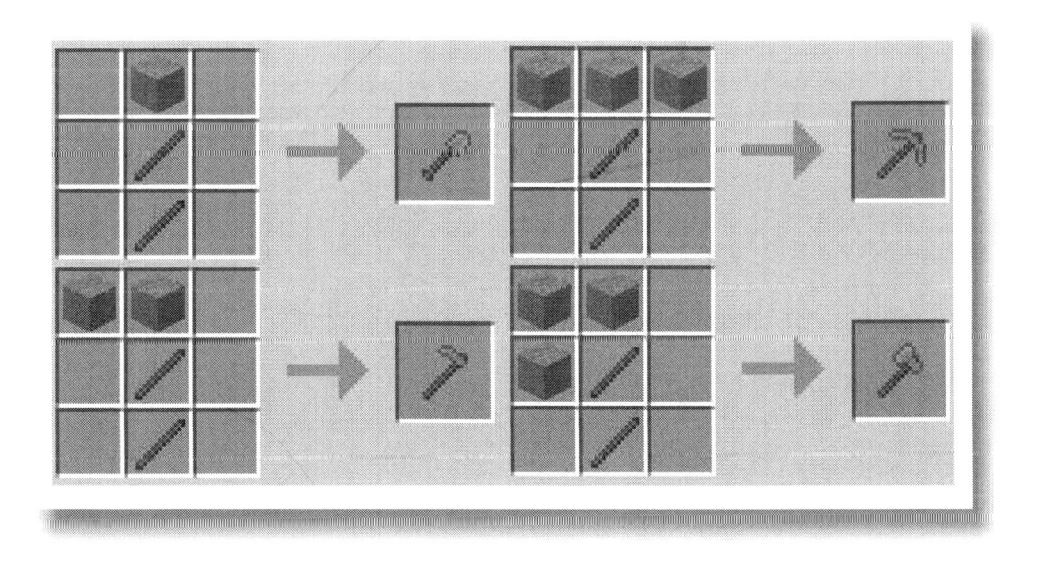

Stone pick axe allows you to mine for better ores which wooden pick axes can't. Moreover, stone swords are better and give more damage to mobs.

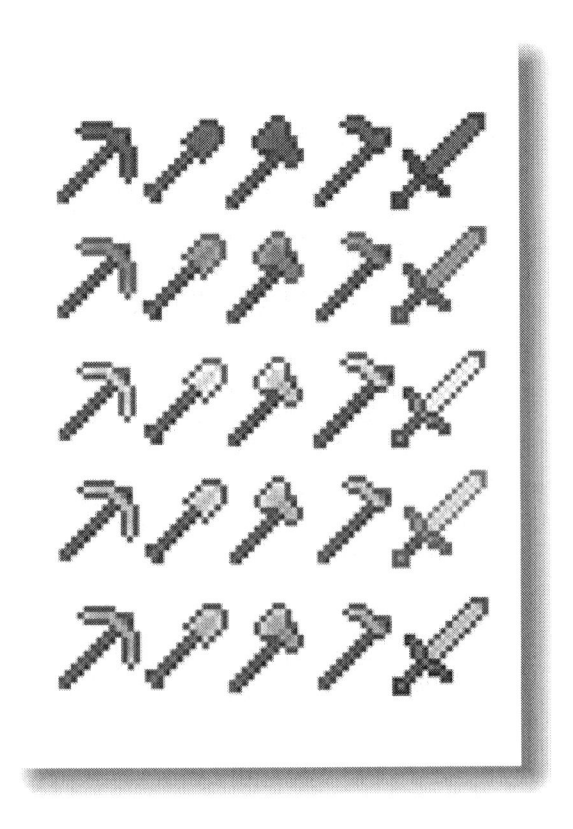

Once you get access to better ores such as tin, iron, silver, gold, diamond and more, you can start crafting better weapons and armor as well.

While armor doesn't protect you 100% from any mob damage, it does greatly reduce it.

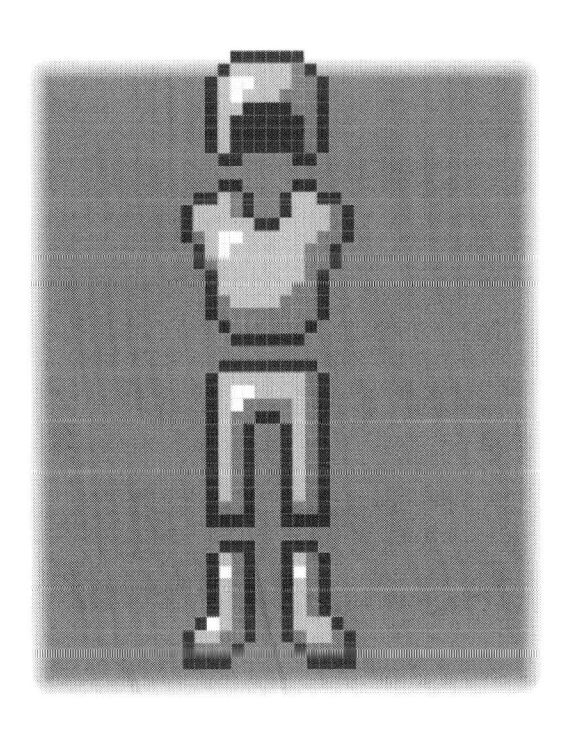

Building Your First Shelter

The first shelter you make in Minecraft does not have to be a work of art. What you want to do is to survive the first night so you get to live to see another day. For this purpose, opt for something which will be sturdy but not something you regret leaving behind.

The best way to make one is to look for a mountain side or a hill and start digging a tunnel which is 3x4 in width and depth.

Do not go into a cave since it increases the chances of getting surprise attacked by mobs that spawn in there.

Once you have dug out a small room in the side of a mountain, craft a wooden door with the wood planks to keep out the mob. If you can't find a hill or mountain to dig into, start digging in the ground.

Follow the same measurements and step inside. Use the dirt blocks you collected to close the opening over your head. Once inside, place a few torches around you and smelt and craft the night away.

You will need to rely on a watch to time the night since being underground will not allow you visually see the day/night cycle happening.

Once its dawn, you can pop out safely from your shelter and gather more resources. However, you might still encounter a few zombies and skeletons but it's best to stay away from them as the sun will burn them.

If they are burning and they touch you, you will catch fire as well. The only way to put it out would be by jumping into water and if there's none nearby, you are going to take a lot of damage.

Other than this factor though, congratulations, you just survived your first night in Minecraft. From now on, it's all smooth sailing! Just keep doing what you're doing and you're good to go!

Happy Mining!

Made in the USA
San Bernardino, CA
28 November 2016